Angelic
Trance
Magick

Ben Woodcroft

TABLE of CONTENTS

Trance Magick

The angelic trance is easy to achieve, and its effects are profound. Follow brief magickal instruction, and your life will change for the better.

It may sound absurd, but I am prepared to say that this is magick that cannot fail. It is the *only* magick I know that cannot fail. The method requires a commitment from you in the form of time and attention, but this is a small price to pay. The trance only takes a few minutes, but if you commit to this magick, changes will come.

You can enter the trance for longer and chain together a sequence of trances for greater change, or you can keep it simple. Whatever way you prefer to work, the angels will cooperate.

Be assured that no great effort is required to achieve the trance state. By using the sigils in this book, you seek the help of angels, and they will ease you into the required trance. From that state, you communicate your needs to the angels. The trance is very light, safe, and not in any way disturbing, so you don't need to worry that you'll have to get completely zoned out. It's much easier than that.

Magick of all kinds can work. A basic spell, invented out of need, can work if you construct it well. Traditional and modern angelic magick often works if you ask for help sincerely. But most magick is subject to some disappointments, and rituals don't always work, or they bring unwanted surprises and disruptions. *This* magick cannot fail because the angels will not refuse to help when you communicate your sincere needs. Your life will begin to transform in ways that benefit you now and in the future.

The magick is also quite different because you do not need to speak any magick words, and you are not required to manipulate or 'fake' your emotions. By showing the angels what you actually feel, whether it is sadness, despair, anxiety, loss, grief, distress, or perhaps a burning desire, you get results.

There is no requirement to imagine or create new feelings. You only show the angels what you feel now, and through the angelic trance, they will guide you to a new state of being that will attract whatever you need to satisfy your desires.

There are many ways to contact angels and ask for help. There are numerous books you can use if you need the help of an angel, with prayers, chants, rituals, and many other methods. I have written two such books myself, called *Angelic Sigils, Seals, and Calls*, and *The Angel Overlords*, and I stand by their power. Using magick to get what you want is a good way to live. It is not the only way to connect with the angels.

The angelic trance creates a state that can provide solutions to everyday problems, and it can also help you deal with your own difficult emotions, any state of fear or suffering, and bring relief to mental and emotional distress. The magickal state is achieved with the aid of the angels, who support your quest for change, and I hope you will soon sense that if you put the smallest faith in the magick, you will be rewarded.

Even the simplest of trance states will help you learn who you are. By exploring who you are, what you need to be happy, how to overcome adversity, and the best way to release your potential, you are set on the path to achieving everything you desire.

This claim is not made boastfully but with surety. It is a claim I am confident in making because I know that if you put in the time to fully explore these angelic trances, you cannot fail but change for the better. As you become more attuned to your true needs, you will draw their reality to you. At times, it will be almost effortless.

You can, of course, use the book to solve problems as needed, but you may find you want to move deeper and discover more. A deeper approach will bring a stream of changes to your life and your world, as though you are performing hundreds of perfectly designed rituals to make changes in your life. With just a few short trances, you can bring a great number of transformations to yourself and your reality.

There may well be a transformation in your life, but this does not mean disruption or calamity. You will never attract anything you don't want, or that isn't right for you now. Of all the magick I have worked with, this is some of the most transformative but also the least disruptive. The change that comes will always feel right for you.

You now understand that this is not a set of spells but a way of using a trance state to communicate with angels. Developed over hundreds of years, from what I can gather from my research, it helps you to achieve a harmony of understanding. This harmony puts you at ease, encourages your inner dreams, and shows you how you can obtain and experience what you want.

It would be an overstatement to say that all your problems will end, all enemies shall be defeated, and that success will be handed to you within weeks. I might sell more copies of the book if I made those claims, but it's imperative for me to be honest. Although results and changes can occur immediately, it is the pleasure of the journey that matters most. When you experience these trances, you will never regret what they have given to you.

Whatever fears prevent you from being who you truly are will be exposed to you and shown for that they are, comfortably and safely, so that you can rise above them. Whatever deep feelings you have, they will be clear, easing pain, guilt, and regret. Whatever experience you seek will be made known to you. There will be no more denying what it is you secretly dream of becoming. This knowledge will empower you to seek what you desire.

The angels do more than reveal yourself to yourself. They show how you can change, what you can do, and how you can walk the path to obtaining everything you need in the easiest way. It would be a cruel magick that revealed your deepest desires and left you with no way to obtain them. Using this trance state, you will gain extreme clarity. You will discover the easiest way to get where you want to be. This discovery will come in a gradual and broadening knowledge and intuition about yourself and the course of your life.

You can use this book once, to solve a problem. Or you may explore it daily to fine-tune the manifestation of your desires. That is your choice.

Many magickal methods are currently about getting what you want, fast, no matter the cost. I hope you will find the time, whether it is now or at some time in the future, to open yourself to the simple methods shown here. When you give your time to this magickal trance of the angels, it will always reward your attention.

Why, though, should you choose to use this book instead of one that you already own? When is it best to use trance magick? When people look to magick, they may think, *give me more money, give me more power, give me more sex.* Well, magick will do that, but I don't think magick is always a simple ordering service. I have found this magick is most effective when you have an extremely deep need. If you just casually want a bit of extra money because it would be fun, it's less likely to work than when you sincerely want more money because there is something you *really* desire. The deeper the need, the more powerful the magick.

This truth can easily be misinterpreted. When I have taught angelic trance magick, I have seen students believe that it can only be used when you are desperate. It is true that it *can* be used when you are desperate, and this makes it very special. There is so much magick that fails when you are desperate. Your desperate need defuses the magickal power. With trance magick, desperation is acceptable. But you don't *need* to be desperate.

Most recently, I taught the method to a young woman who dearly wanted to buy one of the new digital cameras. This wasn't a spiritual need or something required to keep her in business; it was a purely material desire. But it was a strong desire. She is a good photographer, she *loves* cameras, she was limited by her current equipment, and she wanted a camera that was far outside of her price range. The angelic trance was what she needed, and she got what she wanted.

Use this book when your need feels real, rather than casual or optional. When you definitely want something, the magick will work.

This magick is also well-suited to those times when you can't think of a solution. In many situations, you know what you want, and you can take magickal steps to get there. But sometimes, all you know is that you want less anxiety, more wisdom, some peace, a better relationship, or something of that nature. When you have that kind of feeling, this magick is an excellent way of offering your problem to the angels and letting them find a solution for you. The angels can see your possible futures, and when you show them your need, they know the best way to satisfy that need. This doesn't mean you relinquish control of your life, but that you can trust the angels to come up with the best solution to your problem.

If you are unsure about whether or not to use this magick, I suggest you try it anyway. There is no harm in practicing the magick. You will get used to the process, and you may be surprised by some unexpected results.

Trance can occur in just a few moments, so this is not demanding magick. If you feel any excitement about using this book, try it out and see what it can do for you.

The Trance State

You do not need to think of trance as a massively altered state of consciousness. It is an altered state, but you are not completely zoned out, or in the sort of zombie trance you see in the movies. This trance is achieved for the purpose of magick, not for the purpose of being in a trance. You aren't going to lose yourself in ecstasy or strangeness. The effects can be beautiful, but any effects you feel are incidental. You achieve the trance state to attain a desire. As such, you do not need to create a massively changed state of mind. You do not need to work towards a particular state. For some people, there will be a dramatic change in consciousness, and for others, it will feel like nothing has happened. That is how trance is, and that's fine.

Some years ago, I spent some time with several hypnotists, even touring briefly with a professional stage hypnotist. He wasn't very well known, but he could work the audience, and his show was always hilarious. I was fascinated to hear what the audience members experienced when they got up on stage and spent an hour in a hypnotic trance. For so many, they said it was not all that different from ordinary life, but it felt easier to play and pretend. Others said they felt relaxed and dreamy. And some said it was extremely spacey and otherworldly. All of these were genuine trance states.

This makes it very difficult to explain trance or define it in any way. Some people expect it to be like meditation, and others think it will be something closer to a seizure. An example I have always loved is one used by many stage hypnotists. When you watch a movie in a darkened room, if you don't talk or eat and focus only on the story, you enter a trance. You engage with the story, the characters, the emotions. You feel things for characters that are not real. You experience fear, excitement, and you may even cry, all because of things that are being simulated. You forget about the room you are in, and you become at one with the movie. That is a deep trance. In fact, it's probably a deeper trance than you need for magick.

Another example, often cited, is taking a familiar drive. For most people, driving a familiar route happens on automatic. You can daydream, think about things, or think about nothing, all while part of your mind somehow keeps driving the car without you thinking about it or noticing where you are. All of a sudden, you've arrived. That is trance.

There are many volumes written about trance, with many debates about what it is, how it can be achieved, and what it's for. The feeling I get is that trance is a relatively normal and natural state of altered consciousness. It's certainly not ordinary consciousness, but it's not something that's really strange and out there. It's something we do quite often. When we choose to enter a trance, it can be a powerful way to connect with magick.

For the remainder of this book, you do not need to worry about what trance is or isn't. You certainly should never worry about whether you are achieving trance, or getting into a deep enough trance. Follow the instructions, which are easy to follow, and the correct state *will* be achieved. But know, from this point on, you are not trying to create a drug-like zone-out. This book is about angels, and your purpose is to use a level of trance to achieve a connection with angels. Never forget that the angelic magick is your purpose, and any sensation of trance is utterly incidental.

This is a short book with a focus only on the instructions you need to begin the work. I will not explore the background of magick, or trance, in much more detail. A moment of trance will show you more about the potential of the magick than chapters of history or theory.

The magick is safe, and you need no additional protection. In many rituals, there is much preliminary work, calling out names of God and preparing the magickal space. You do not need to do that here. Each trance ritual is a self-contained process that brings its own protection. If you are disturbed briefly by somebody walking by, or a loud noise, the trance is not so delicate that it will shatter. You continue, and the trance continues. But if you stop to chat or glance down at your phone, that will not work. You will need to keep your mind on the magick, but this doesn't require a super-human level of concentration.

I believe the method was developed to be self-working. That is, the act of following the instructions makes you able to concentrate. If that sounds too abstract, you should understand what I mean when you do the work, and trance happens quite effortlessly.

For each angel, there is a simple sigil. This is nothing more than a circle with the angel's name. The name is written vertically, using one of the angelic alphabets. I am aware that there are much prettier sigils, but this is not about aesthetics. (The actual sigils do not contain arrows, of course, and these are for illustration only.)

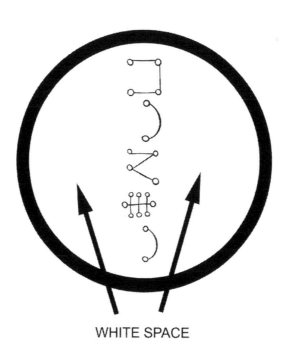

WHITE SPACE

The purpose of a sigil is to focus your attention toward an angel, and in some cases, to soften the ordinary barrier of existence, to make the connection easier. It has been said, quite correctly, that you could write an angel's name in a circle, in English, focus on it, and you would get a result. That *is* a sigil. But there are benefits to using other signs and symbols, and here, the vertical arrangement assists the trance. This particular celestial alphabet has been found to be the most effective.

You can see white space on either side of the vertical name, indicated by the arrows. To achieve trance, you move your eyes from the space on the left, over to the space on the right, and back again. You do this slowly and gently, not moving your head, just moving your eyes from side to side. Repeating this eye movement over the sigil activates the trance state.

My understanding is that this eye movement serves two purposes. The first is to enable the angelic name to be absorbed by your inner self. You are not looking at it directly, and so it moves into your subconscious for the duration of the ritual. Your connection to the angel is instantaneous, whether you feel it or not. The second reason is that this eye movement is known to create a more open state of consciousness. This has been known by occultists, visionaries, and mystics for centuries, and is even being integrated into some modern psychological practices to encourage psychological openness and flexibility.

You may be worried about how fast to move your eyes, or how slowly, or how much they should move, or how close the book should be to your eyes. I know, from teaching this to many students, that as soon as I describe the technique, they worry they will get it wrong. Once again, you cannot get this wrong if you follow one rule. Do what feels comfortable.

You are not trying to *make* yourself go into an altered state of consciousness by moving your eyes around until you get dizzy or feel strange. That would be counter-productive. Allow whatever occurs to occur. Move your eyes as slowly as you like, without strain, and so there is no discomfort.

An altered state may occur, where you begin to sense the magick arising and feelings coming to you, but this is not essential. The trance may not feel strong or noticeable, and that is fine because your purpose is not to feel strange but to activate magick. You are allowing the absorption of the letters without a direct focus on them. It doesn't matter if you do look at the letters, but overall, you are trying to create a rhythm. It's a sort of tick-tock, from side to side, across the sigil.

If you find you cannot perform the eye movements without feeling discomfort, then you can slow it right down. If you *can* do the eye movement successfully, with a tick-tock rhythm, that is the best way, and most people have no problem with it.

I move my eyes slowly, taking about one second to move from one side of the sigil to the other. The sigil is at arm's length. I move my eyes smoothly, rather than jerking them from one side to the other. That is comfortable for me. You will discover what is comfortable for you, and whatever that is will be the right way for you to achieve the trance.

That is the technique. If you choose any sigil in the book and move your eyes in that way, after a few seconds, you will begin to enter the trance state. You are free to do this without any direct intention, practicing without purpose or desire, but only if you want to get used to the method. This is not essential, and you can move straight into a ritual without any practice.

It is possible you will achieve a higher state of consciousness, and it is possible you will sense the angel's presence, but please do not be surprised if you feel nothing more than relaxed. If you perform this eye movement over a sigil for just a few moments, trance will have been achieved whether you feel it or not.

The Angelic Trance Ritual

There are more details coming up on how to choose the right power and how to develop this magick, but I would like to describe the ritual itself. This way, you understand what you will be doing, and the rest of the book should make more sense.

The instructions are brief, but this is all you require to get the trance to connect you to the angels. When I've taught this privately or in workshops, I've often seen students make the assumption that this is just the first step when it's actually the whole ritual.

I would normally suggest finding a place where you can be alone and undisturbed, but in some cases, you may choose to use this magick in the midst of turmoil. I know this has been used successfully by anxious flyers, who have sought the power of Elemiah to *Ease Anxiety* during take-off. It can be profoundly and immediately effective.

The magick can be used at the last moment before something dramatic is about to happen, or when you're in the midst of a crisis. If you are driven by need, the ritual can be performed anywhere.

Most often, I expect you will use it in calm privacy, with an overview of your needs, and in a place where you can easily focus. That's what I'll describe now, but remember that the sigils *can* be accessed and used to create a brief trance in the middle of more dramatic events, if you have a moment to spare.

The problem you are trying to solve, or the result you are seeking, will be clear to you. It might be held in your mind as an image, a phrase, or just a jumble of thoughts. You do not need to focus on this in great detail, but remind yourself of why you are doing the ritual and what you hope to achieve. This takes only a few seconds but is vital.

You now move your eyes over the sigil as described earlier, from one side to the other. As you continue to do this, the trance state will evolve. Do not focus on whether or not you are in a trance.

If you feel that the effects are too intense at any time, you can stop, but it is rare for people to feel anything other than pleasant sensations. If you sense the presence of the angel, you can welcome that feeling, but you do not need to give thanks or aim to communicate with the angel. If you cannot feel the angel's reality at all, let that be as it is, and carry on anyway.

If you feel absolutely nothing, that is always fine, and you may find that far from feeling trance-like, your mind begins to run with all sorts of random thoughts. This is often part of the process of settling into the trance state. You are not meditating, so there is no need to empty your mind.

Although you are not trying to empty your mind, the next step is to bring your attention to your problem or desire. There is no need to generate strong feelings, either positive or negative. Instead, just remember your problem or desire. You're performing magick to achieve something, to change something, so think about what it is. Think about it as you continue to move your eyes.

By doing this, you offer your problem or desire to the angel, and in offering it, you are requesting help. You do not need to ask for help directly or use any words. By thinking about your problem or desire, while in the trance, you *are* seeking help.

I have said that you do not need to feel anything, and if you go through this whole process without feeling any emotions, that is not a problem. If you feel strong negative emotions about the problem, you may find they change or shift, or that insights come to you. If you are seeking immediate relief from a feeling such as grief or anxiety, you should expect some relief, which grows over the coming minutes. But if nothing happens at first, don't despair, as results will come at varying speeds.

The magick is highly adaptable, and it can be used to bring relief in the moment, or to ask for life-changing shifts in your reality. You might seek something as direct as relief from

22

depression, or you might be asking for a career change. The scale of your problem or desire does not matter, only that you sincerely desire change.

If you're worried about what to think or how to think it, you're too worried about the process. If you have chosen to perform a ritual, you know what your problem or desire is. You know what you want to change. Whether you think about it as a phrase, an image, a word, or just a vague feeling, that is all you need to bring to mind.

You might find yourself feeling tearful, desperate, or as though you're pleading for help. That is fine. In many forms of magick, you command angels or ask them directly or forcibly to help you. Here, you *are* asking for help, and if you feel like you are pleading for help, that is understandable. Many times, you will not feel that way at all, and that is also fine.

The only challenge with this magick is knowing when to stop. A simple solution is to perform this for three minutes and then stop, knowing that is long enough. Or if you feel that you've been heard by the angel, you can stop sooner, even if the ritual has only taken a few seconds. Once the angel has heard you clearly, there is no need to continue. Your only purpose is to use trance to convey your need, so once you have been heard, you can stop. It might take less than half a minute, or it might take up to three minutes.

You may not be able to sense when the angel has heard you. Some people have no problem with this and can always feel that their problem has been lifted away and is being handled by the angels. Other people do not sense this at all. If you feel nothing, perform the magick for about three minutes. This will ensure that you've been heard because it never takes longer than that. If you want a sure-fire way to know you've completed the ritual, perform it for three minutes.

If, however, you find that you sense something, where you feel like the angel has heard you, trust that feeling and stop. Either method will work.

To stop the ritual, all you do is stop moving your eyes and close the book.

If you are looking to experience deep trance states that last much longer for some other purpose, I will cover that in a later part of the book. For obtaining magickal results and change, you will only need a short ritual.

Students frequently ask how often they need to perform a trance ritual to obtain a result, and the answer is entirely dependent upon the circumstances. If you are seeking to manifest a specific result, performing the ritual once is enough. When you perform a ritual for immediate relief from a feeling, you may then call the same angel at another time, asking for more long-term relief. With the example of anxious flyers, you could seek help in the moment, but then at a later date, ask the angel to remove your fear of flying.

The magick is adaptable, and I know that some people will use the trance to connect with the power of Creativity and Inspiration before writing or painting. Others will perform quite general rituals to improve finances and business, and will then use more specific rituals to confront and ease each problem as it arises, or to attract more money where needed. I believe this is a good approach.

If you want to perform a ritual more than once, you can enter the trance state as often as you want, but it is not required. I know some people like to perform a ritual three times, just to make sure they've been heard, and if you choose this path, that is fine and may reassure you, but I believe you will soon find that once is enough.

You may perform the ritual once and find that a few days later, the problem begins to resolve, but some new issues arise. You might perform the ritual again, to tackle the new version of the problem. In truth, this is not a case of repeating the ritual but adapting the ritual as the problem changes. You may continue in this way for some time with extremely complicated problems, but you will find the results make it worthwhile.

Results may be immediate and obvious, or they may be much less obvious and take longer to develop. If it feels like your trance has not brought the change you seek, see the later chapter on combining rituals. Often, one slight change to another aspect of your life can help release a flood of magickal change.

You can use the angelic trance while you are using other forms of magick, and you may use it to add power to other workings. I prefer to use this magick by itself, in times of greater need and when desires are especially strong.

There is no limit on the number of rituals you can perform in a day, but I doubt any experienced occultist would recommend a flood of magick. In rare cases, this can work, but normally, it dilutes your intentions and your ability to remain intuitively aware of potential changes. Use the magick as often as you like, but consider that moderation may be more effective than excess.

The method is simple. Remind yourself why you are asking for a result. Move your eyes over the sigil, and after a few seconds, begin to think about your problem or desire. Accept whatever you think or feel. Bring your attention back to the problem or desire as you continue to move your eyes. When you feel you've been heard, or when three minutes have gone by, stop moving your eyes, and the ritual is complete. I trust that you will find great power here, despite the simplicity, and I invite you to explore and experiment.

Understanding The Powers

Magickal discoveries are made, and then sometimes they are forgotten or set aside, despite their importance. I believe that what I am about to cover is known by most occultists and many readers of occult books, but it is surprisingly neglected. This simple truth is that *any* angel you choose can grant you the results you require.

In almost all occult books or magickal grimoires, each angel is listed along with a description of its specific powers. If you want to access those powers, you choose that angel. Even this book does that, although to a lesser extent. And after some time, we all come to believe that one angel is the best for dealing with relationship problems, while another is perfect for prosperity. In practice, there is some truth to this, and that is why all our books are written that way. The angels do seem to excel in certain areas, but this may be because of our expectations.

When your need is very deep, real, and extremely important to you, *any* angel will do the work. This means that if you bring great need and sincerity to the magick, asking for what you really need, any angel could respond.

When I was told of this fact, my first question was why I needed seventy-two angels if one could do what I wanted? The answer is complicated, but a simplified version of it is to say that there *are* seventy-two angels, regardless of your needs, and you can call one, many, or all of them.

With this in mind, I will say that you can use any angel in this book for any purpose, and if your needs are great, you will see a response from that angel. Approach the angel with the feeling of sincere need, and you will not be ignored. When would you do this? If you simply cannot decide which angel would be best for your needs, then choose any. It will work.

Why, then, go to the trouble of choosing an angel? I believe that choosing an angel that is closely aligned to your needs, according to the expected benefits, can improve the results. More importantly, the act of choosing an angel is a part of the process. When you go to the trouble of choosing an angel, doing so helps you understand your needs, seeing your problem from several angles. This brief contemplation can be powerful. Every time you have a problem that needs solving, see if you can find an angel (or a combination of angels) that could help. Most of the time, you will find the angel or angels you need. If not, do what I say above, and use any angel to seek your result.

As you look through the book, you may think I have made this difficult for you by describing the angels' powers so briefly. This brevity should, in fact, help you.

I'll elaborate on this briefly to put you at ease. In most modern magick books, you find the angel's name, followed by a list of its powers, and often, a brief paragraph summarising what these powers can do. This can be undeniably useful. But also, these paragraphs can sometimes be limiting. What I have done for you in this book, with the guidance of the angels and many years of experience, is to describe the powers as briefly as possible. And the briefer the description, the more scope it has to help you.

As an example, there is the angel Machiel. In this book, I simply say, *Machiel: Popularity*. In a more conventional grimoire, I might have given a few examples about how this power can help improve your popularity in social situations, as well as at work. But think about what popularity actually means. There are *thousands* of examples. You could use this power to be more popular on social media. The power could be used to gain new readers if you are an author. The power could help you expand your business networks by being popular at conferences. There are, quite literally, thousands of ways you can interpret this power, depending on your life and your needs. And that is what you must do. For each power, *you interpret the words*.

When you see *Kahetel: Counteract Evil*, you may wonder what kind of evil this counteracts. Is it for stopping evil curses, or supernatural presences, or evil people? The answer is that whatever you perceive as evil can be counteracted. You might even be fighting an inner evil, some vice or habit that you perceive to be an evil part of yourself. Personally, I would not regard an inner problem to be evil, but if *you* do, the magick can work to counteract that evil. I hope this illustrates that your interpretation of the powers is what counts. There is almost unlimited potential when you allow yourself to interpret the powers.

You may also wonder whether the magick is only about affecting yourself or whether it can affect others. In most cases, magick always affects something within you, something in other people, while influencing fortune and coincidence in your favour. But you can use this magick on yourself and other people. A power such as *Encourage Love* from the angel Lelahel could be used to encourage somebody to love you, or to help you reconnect with old feelings of love for a partner, or to encourage people to love your creative work, or even to love the tasks you perform for an employer.

Whatever you decide about a power will be right. Whatever the words mean to you will be correct. You cannot go wrong if you put in the effort to understand what the words mean. And you can know that as you seek answers, the angels will sense you reaching for those answers, and they will guide you. The magick begins when you begin to contemplate the powers.

When reading through the book casually, you may speculate about the powers with some interest, but when you have a burning desire, you will speculate in quite a different manner. When your need is strong, your understanding will be deeper.

I will say this once more to ensure that it cannot be misunderstood. When you seek to understand an angel's powers, you cannot interpret them incorrectly. If you believe a power can work for you in a certain way, it can work that way.

This does not mean you can exaggerate the powers. If an angel can help support or improve a situation, that is one thing, but magick will rarely solve all your problems overnight or make you an instant success. Magick responds to your needs, your sincere desires, and builds on the work you do to resolve your problems. Although results will sometimes occur without any effort on your part, you should assume that the magick always amplifies your own efforts, bringing fortune to everything you do in that area.

I will cover the origin of the angel names briefly, at this point, because what appears here is different from what you may find elsewhere, and it can help to understand a small amount of background material. I will give you no more than what you need.

These angel names have many histories and apparent origins, but it's also interesting to note they are encoded in the Bible. There are three verses of Exodus (being 14: 19-21) that, when written in a certain pattern, create The 72 Names of God, such as Vehu, Elem, and Lelah.

When you take these names and ad El or Iah to the end, you create an angel name. Using those examples, you would get Vehuiah, Elemiah, and Lelahel. These names mean, Vehu of God, Elem of God, and Lelah of God. There are seventy-two of these angels in total.

There is some debate about which ending each angel name should use, and you will find the names are often spelled quite differently from book to book. This is because the original language was Hebrew, and the vowel sounds are rarely included, which has led to countless interpretations when the words are written in English. You will find, for example, that the angel Veshariah is also known as Vasariah and Vesherel, while Eladiah is also known as Aladiah and Eladel. You can be assured that whatever you use will work, and with this book, you do not need to say the angel's name anyway. The angel's name is written in an angelic script, and so it cannot be wrong.

In previous works, I have chosen to use the El ending for every angel name. In this book, I am using sigils from a slightly different tradition and accessing slightly different powers, and so the names are different, often using the Iah ending. Whatever names you use, you are contacting the correct angels.

When you study the sigil, you will see that sometimes the number of letters in the sigil does not match the number of letters in the name. Again, this is because there are few vowels in the original names. For the angel Vehuiah, for example, the actual letters in the sigil are VHVIH. The sigils use an angelic alphabet to display the name, and you are given an English interpretation of the name that should be easy for you to read.

The powers I list are quite different from those found in other books. If you use other books successfully, including my own, and want to use trance rituals to obtain the powers found in those books, you can try. That approach is often successful. But I recommend that when using the angelic trance, you use the powers listed here when you can.

Combining Powers

What I have described so far is usually all you will need. You perform one angelic trance ritual, and your result will occur when needed. Sometimes, there may be resistance to change, either from within yourself or from external sources, and you may need to work on your problem from a few different angles.

I will give you a brief example and then trust that you can adapt the concept to meet your own needs.

Imagine you are running a business and a competitor has launched a competing product. This is such a serious problem that it threatens to put you out of business. There are so many ways you might choose to handle this problem, but in this example, I will say that you first choose to ease the impact of the competitor's move, then regain your stability, find inspiration for a new idea, and then fund the required changes.

Having made that decision, you might work with Mebahel to *Slow Your Competitors*. Even though they have made their move, this will prevent them from moving too quickly against you. It may also slow their ability to promote their product. The next day you might perform a ritual with Nitel to regain an inner sense of *Stability* so that your emotions don't guide your reactions. On the same day, you might also ask Anuel to *Protect Your Business*. This not only protects your business but increases your calm sense of stability, which will be so important if you are to respond wisely. Seeking inspiration for your next move, you might consider a ritual with Yezalel for *Inspiration*, but you sense this is more about solving problems than seeking new ideas, so you turn to Chavuiah for *Inspired Solutions*, with your focus on discerning a move that will counter your competitor. With your new idea in place, you ask Yeyayel for *Business Fortune* so that your next move is well funded and supported.

As you can imagine, there are many more steps you could take and many alternate paths that would work. For some people, *Protect Your Business* would be enough. Others might immediately seek to *Find Peace in Troubled Times* and then move straight to *Clear Thoughts Under Pressure*.

In most cases, a single ritual can bring the results you want. You might perform *Ease a Crisis* and leave it at that for a while, letting the angels use *their* wisdom. But as you can see, combining rituals can be an intense and satisfying way to direct your magick. With each ritual only taking a few minutes, it can feel empowering to know you are tackling a problem on all fronts.

Although I have given an example about business, it doesn't take much imagination to see how easily this could be adapted to *any* situation, whether it's about family problems, seeking a new relationship, or trying to attract enough money to buy something you desire. When combined wisely, the power of these trance rituals can be genuinely intense. Do not think, however, that you must always combine rituals in this way. If you are able to trust an angel and communicate your desire in a single trance ritual, do so. If you sense there is more that needs to be tackled, use this method. But do not try to micromanage every aspect of a situation every time due to a fear that anything else will fail. This magick responds to trust, so trust it as well as you can.

I will now cover two other ways you can use this magick. I understand that many people will be drawn to this book because they are seeking magickal trance states. I have encountered many students who earnestly want to attain a state of trance but then have difficulty explaining why. Often, it seems, they are seeking an altered state of consciousness that is similar to a dream or something induced by a drug. And sometimes, they are seeking a form of enlightenment. Sometimes it is nothing more than curiosity, wondering what would happen if they stayed in the trance for an hour.

I am not against experimentation, and if you wish to enter the trance for a long period of time, you can. I do not recommend doing this when you are seeking a result, as described earlier. If you enter the trance and communicate your problem, then the ritual is over, and sustaining it is pointless. You can, however, choose to connect with an angel in the trance state without any designated purpose. When you do, it is possible that you will experience some form of deeply altered consciousness, a degree of insight, or something like enlightenment. I make no promises about these experiments as I find they are highly dependent on expectation, willingness to change, innate imagination, and ability to remain focussed. If you wish to experiment, then there is nothing more to this than moving your eyes over the sigil and letting yourself become aware of the angel. No harm can come from this, but I will admit that you may find you have wasted an hour. I hope not, but it's a fair warning.

There is one final way to combine the powers, and this is known as *The Chain of Trance*.

I do not recommend using *The Chain of Trance* for your first ritual. It is a long-term project that can have a potent effect, but I would strongly recommend that you become familiar with the more basic rituals first.

The Chain of Trance is based on the principle that every angel is capable of solving your problem. Instead of asking one angel for help, you ask them all. This means that every angel will help in the best way that they can.

The Chain of Trance is best used only when there is an area of your life that seemingly refuses to change. If you can never start a good relationship, always struggle with debt, or find it impossible to progress in your career, that can be a good time to try this magick.

The process is simple enough, although it is quite demanding. Each day, for seventy-two days, you perform the same ritual, starting with the first angel and working your way through the book. About two and a half months later, you will have offered your problem or desire to every angel in the book. What usually happens is that you notice a change after a few days. Some people then abandon the *Chain*, and that is fine, as they have obtained their desire. Some people adjust the request to take into account the changes that have occurred. In some cases, you may find that even though things are improving, the problem remains fundamentally the same, and so you continue with the magick. All these approaches can work.

Performing *The Chain of Trance* is not overly-demanding and will not cause disruption, but I have seen it cause frustration. The most disappointing case is when you perform this for seventy-two days, and after all that effort, you still feel that nothing has happened. In such cases, I can only recommend that patience can be rewarding, and if you give the magick time to manifest in some way, changes are certain to occur. Remain aware of subtle changes, opportunities, clues about what to do next, and trust your intuition. When change is offered, accept the opportunity to change, and the magick may begin to flow.

This chapter is about exceptions to the rule, and most of the time, you can perform the magick as described earlier, with just one ritual for each situation. If you don't need to make things more complicated, then be happy that you can keep it simple.

The 72 Sigils of Trance

You have prepared fully by reading all that has gone before, and you are now about to come to the angels, their sigils, and the listing of powers.

When you are looking for a specific angel or a particular power, the table of contents will guide you.

If you are using the eBook, one sigil will appear on each page. This book has been mastered in high quality, so the sigils may appear quite large. On some digital reading devices, the sigils may appear to be missing due to their large size, so please reduce the image size if required.

In the paperback, the sigils are presented on all the pages. If you find it distracting having a second sigil within view, you can cover it with your hand or a piece of paper, but this is not required. I have often performed this magick with sigils scattered all over my desk.

1. Vehuiah: Willpower

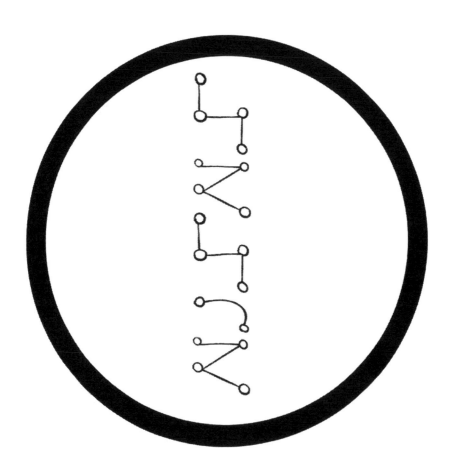

2. Yeliel: Emotional Peace

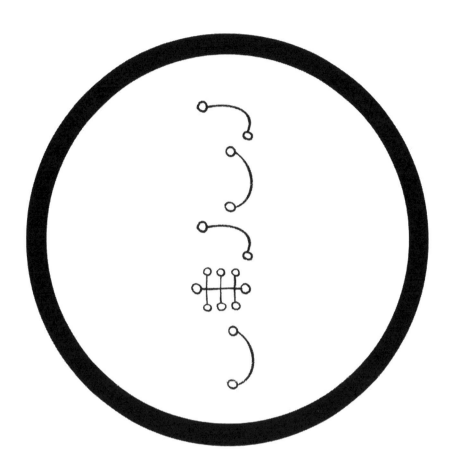

3. Sitael: Emotional Protection

4. Elemiah: Ease Anxiety

5. Mahasiah: Learn Easily

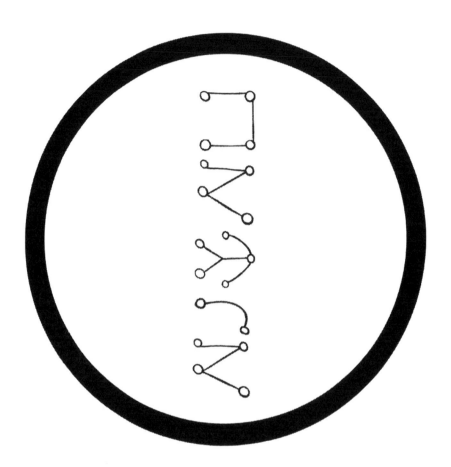

6. Lelahel: Encourage Love

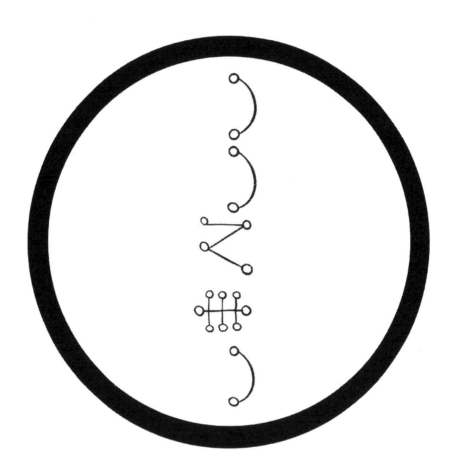

7. Achaiah: Improve Reputation

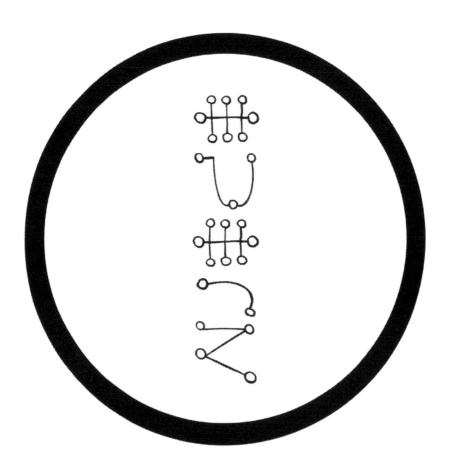

8. Kahetel: Counteract Evil

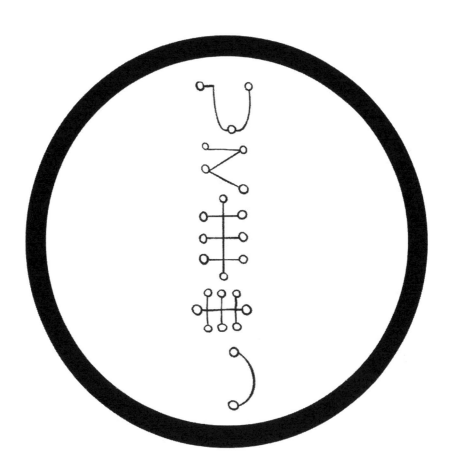

9. Heziel: Friendship

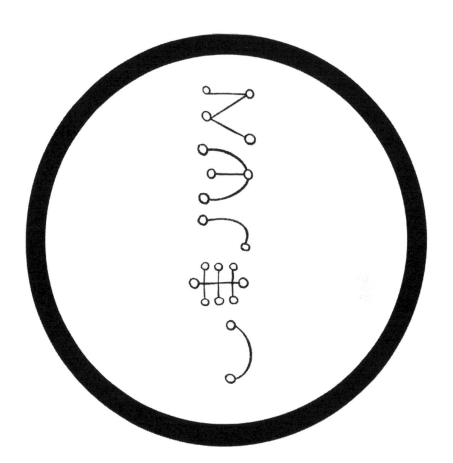

10. Eladiah: Healing

11. Laviah: Victory

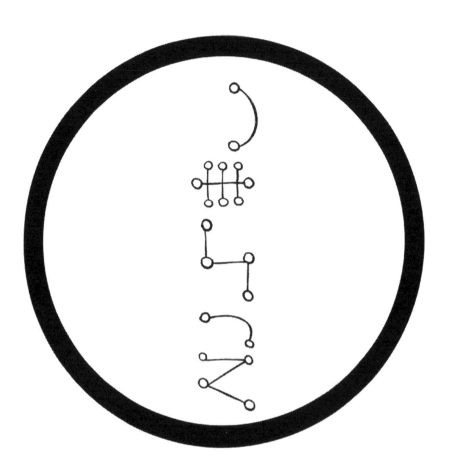

12. Hahaiah: Ease Adversity

13. Yezalel: Inspiration

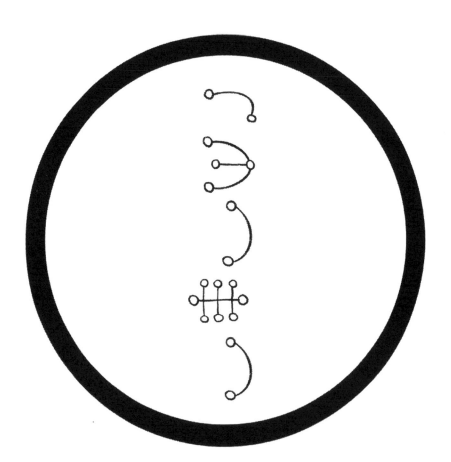

14. Mebahel: Slow Your Competitors

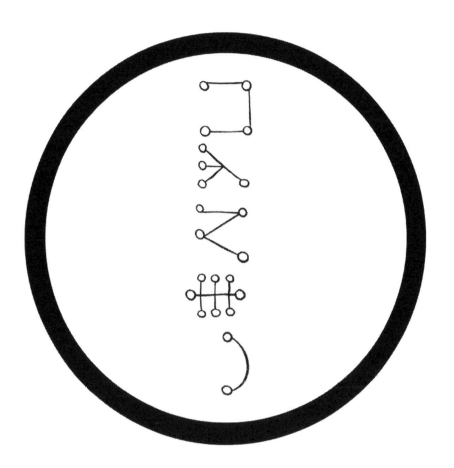

15. Hariel: Peaceful Resolution

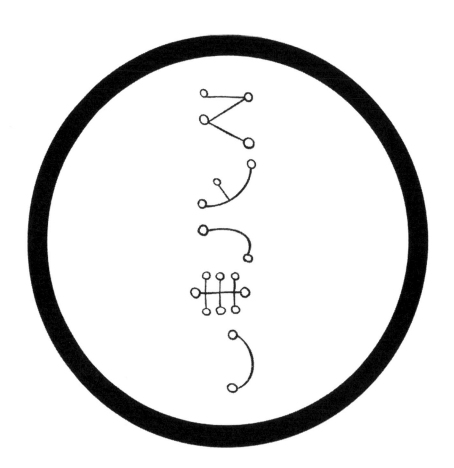

16. Hakemiah: Clear Communication

17. Lavel: Ease Depression

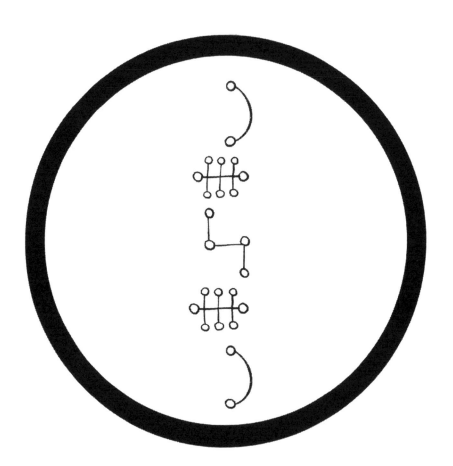

18. Keliel: Legal Dominance

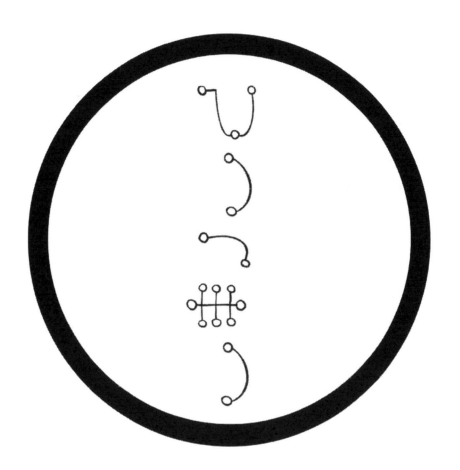

19. Loviah: Make Good Decisions

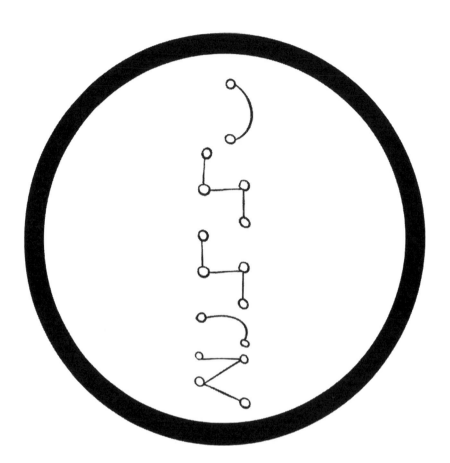

20. Pahaliah: Overcome Addiction

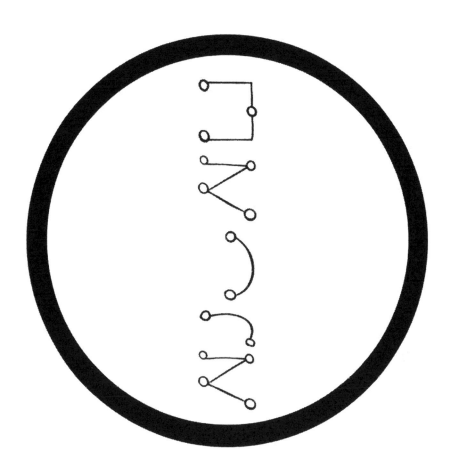

21. Nelakael: Silence Enemies

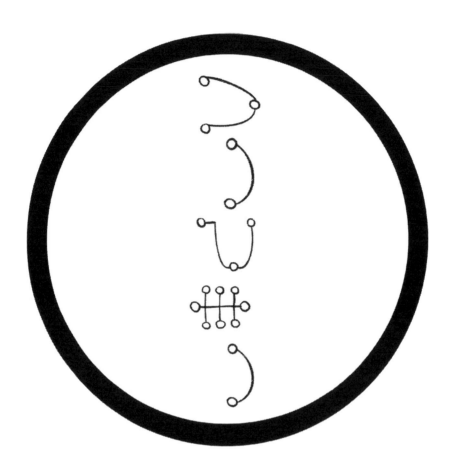

22. Yeyayel: Business Fortune

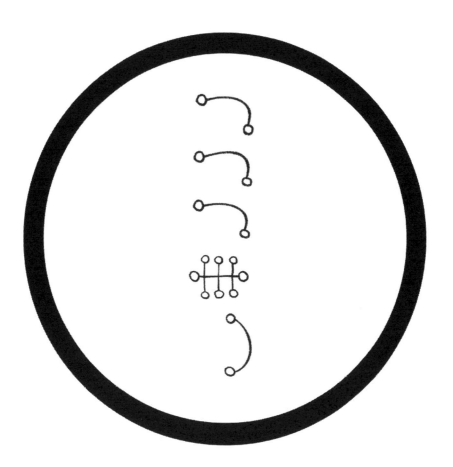

23. Melahel: Overcome Illness

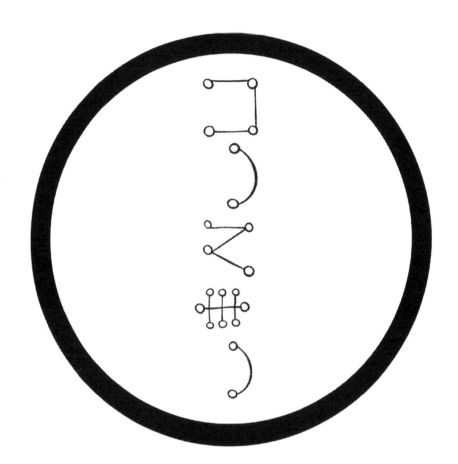

24. Chahuiah: Protect the Home

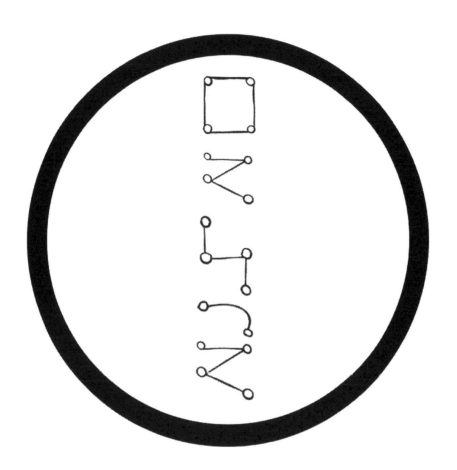

25. Netahiah: Wisdom

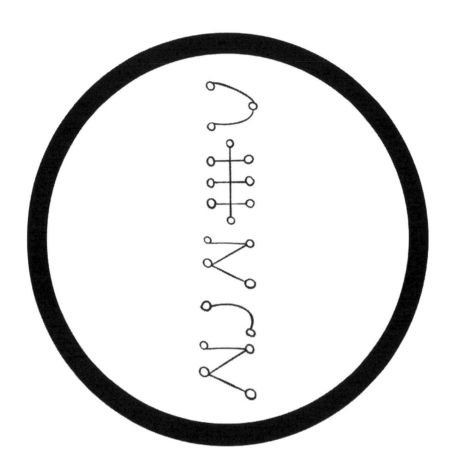

26. Haael: Courage

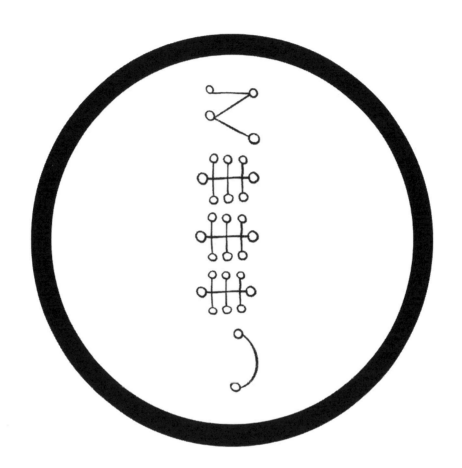

27. Yeretel: Calm Anger and Aggression

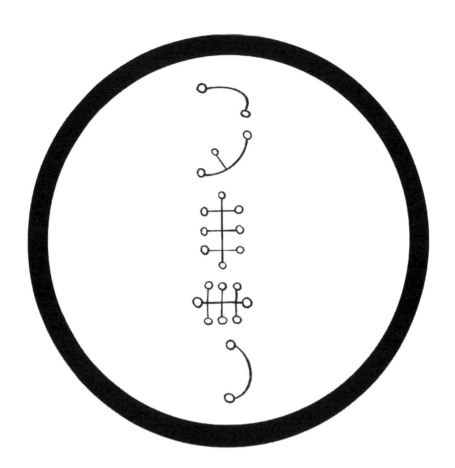

28. Shahahiah: Ease a Crisis

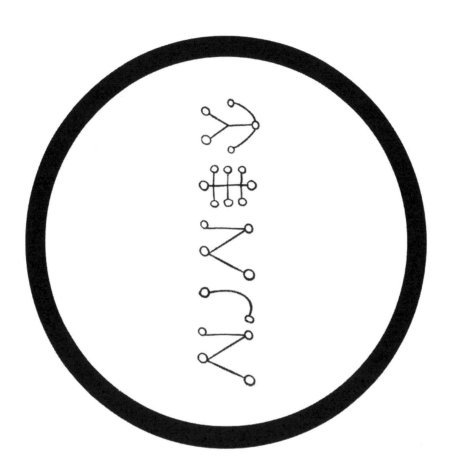

29. Riyiel: Discover Enemies

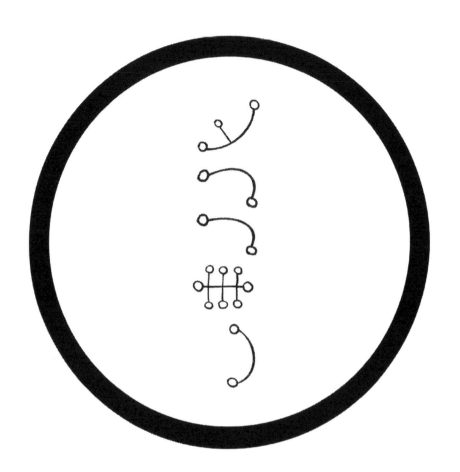

30. Omael: Patience

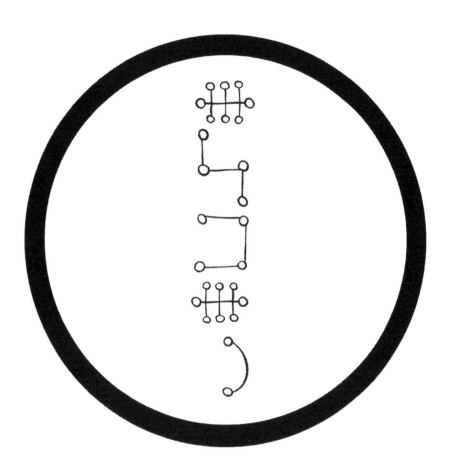

31. Lekavel: Inspired Work

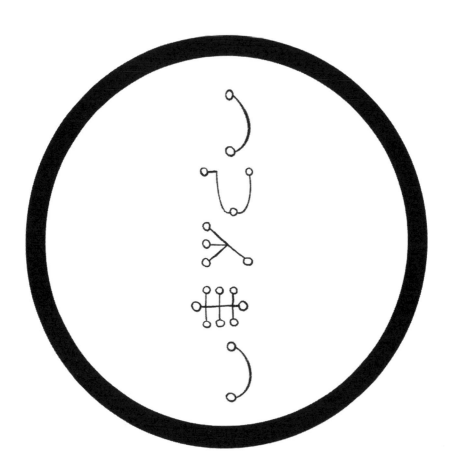

32. Veshariah: Creativity

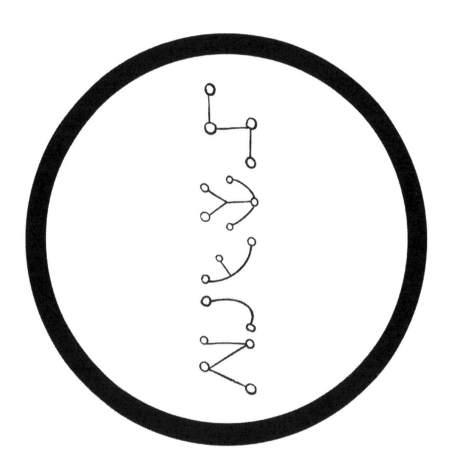

33. Yehuiah: Prove Innocence

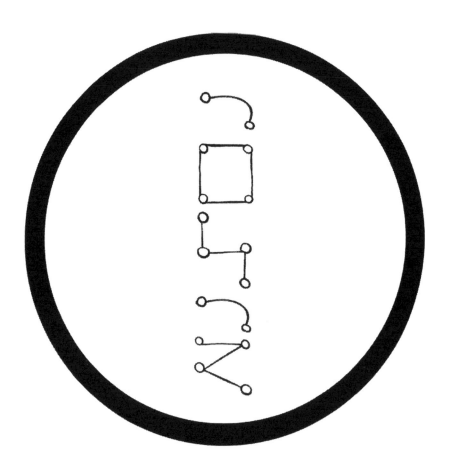

34. Lehachiah: Ease Inner Turmoil

35. Kevekiah: Forgiveness

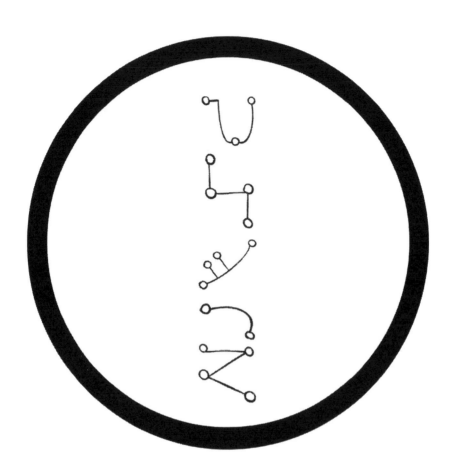

36. Menadel: Project Importance

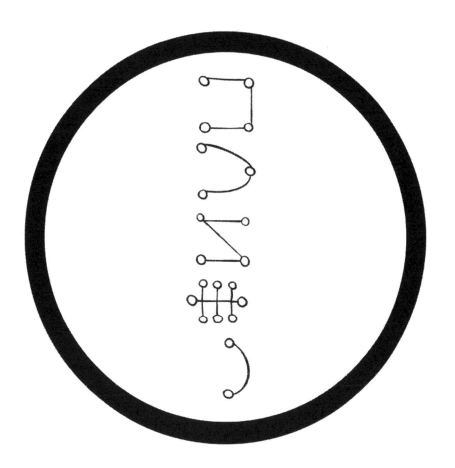

37. Aniel: Calm Reflection

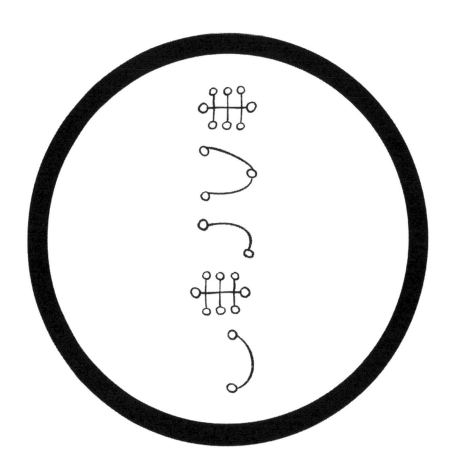

38. Chaamiah: Perceive Truth

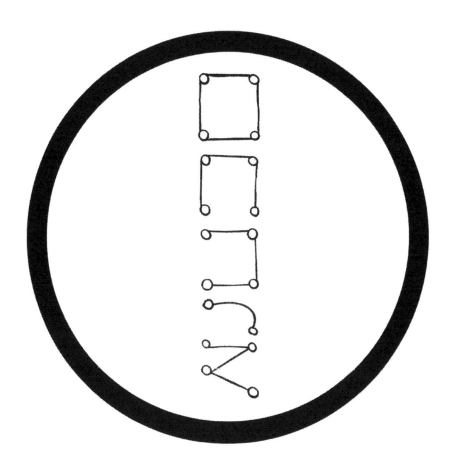

39. Rehoel: Recover Vitality

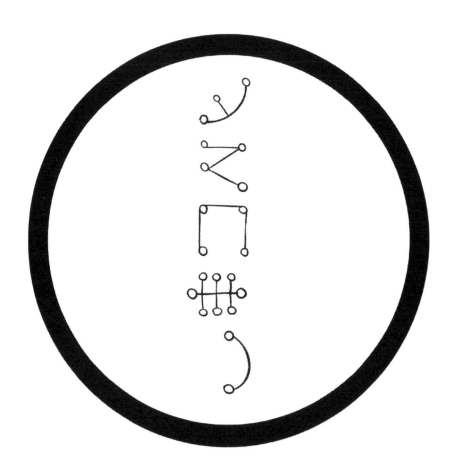

40. Yeyizel: Protect Good Health

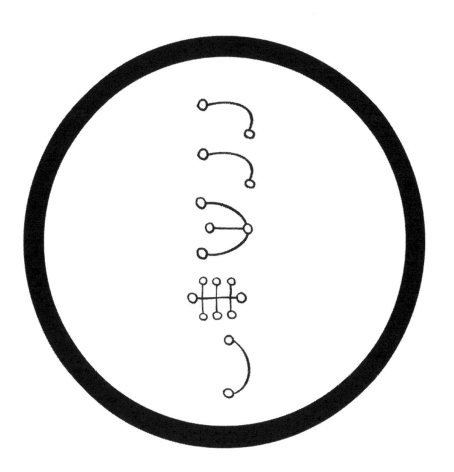

41. Hahahel: Overcome Shame

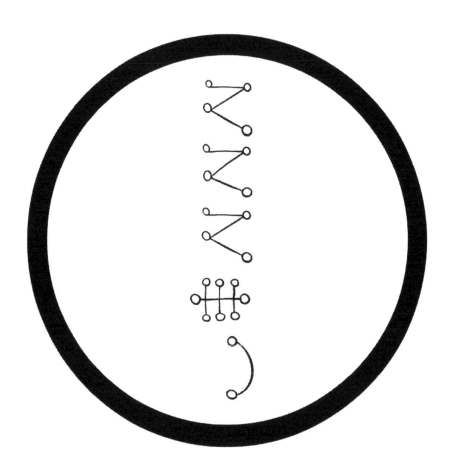

42. Mikael: Protect Against The Powerful

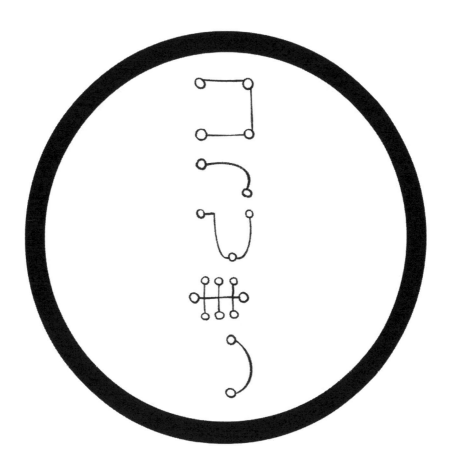

43. Vevaliah: Prosperity

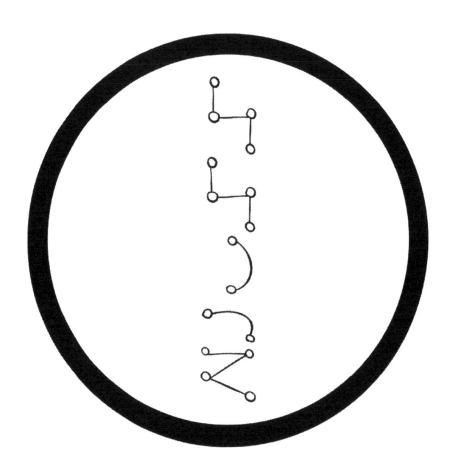

44. Yelahiah: Social Confidence

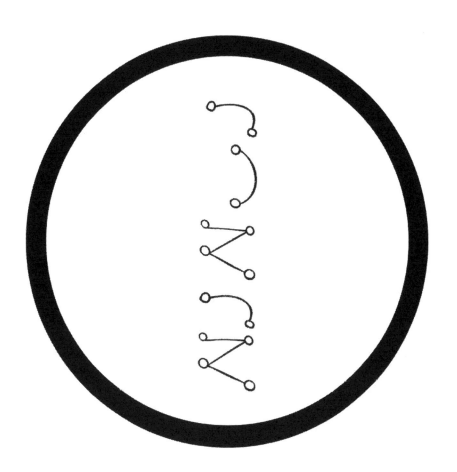

45. Sealiah: Discover Allies

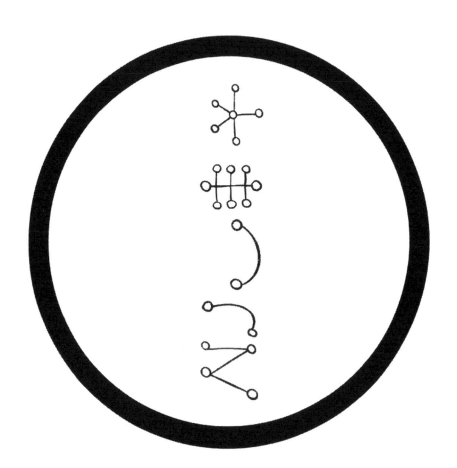

46. Ariel: Improve Finances

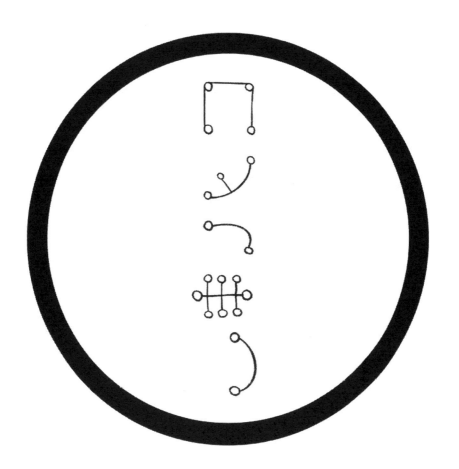

47. Eshaliah: Sense The Future

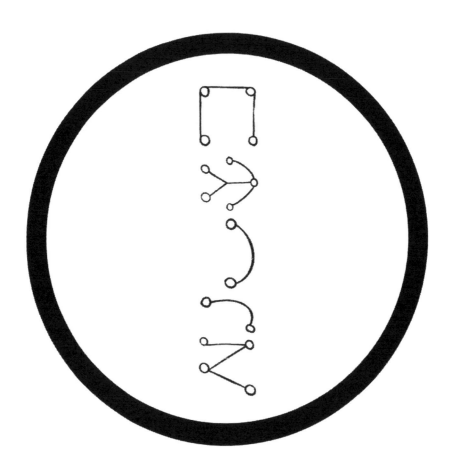

48. Mihel: Strengthen Love

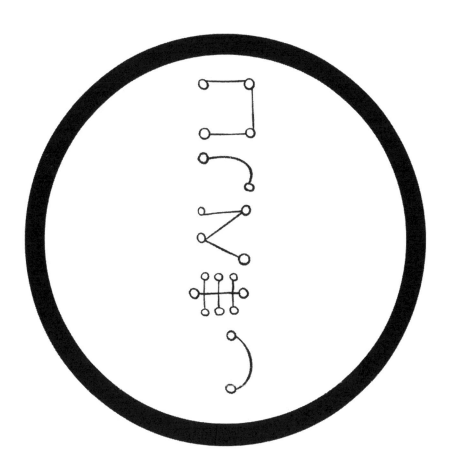

49. Vehuel: Find Peace in Troubled Times

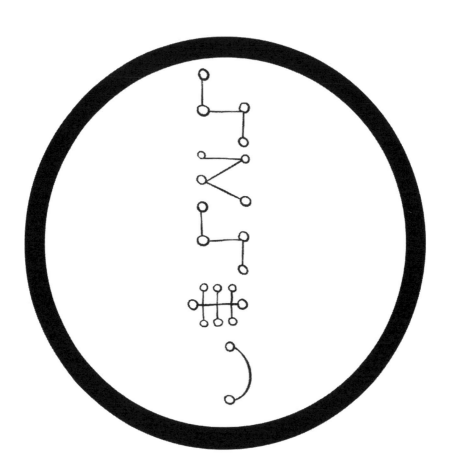

50. Daniel: Legal Justice

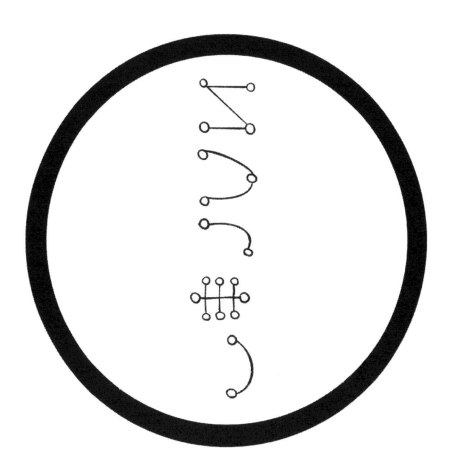

51. Hachashiah: Clear Thoughts Under Pressure

52. Omemiah: Understand a Situation

53. Nenael: Improve Skills

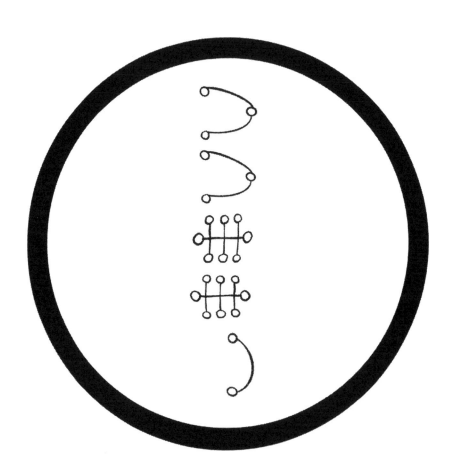

54. Nitel: Stability

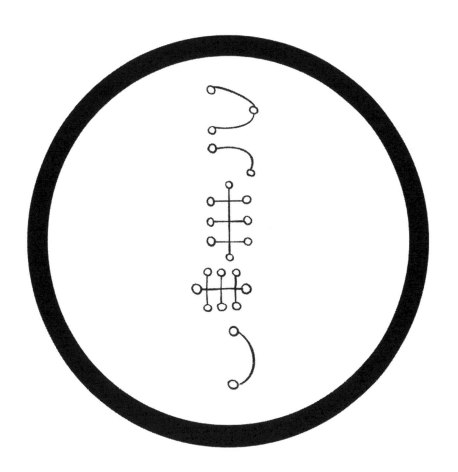

55. Mivahiah: Ease Pain

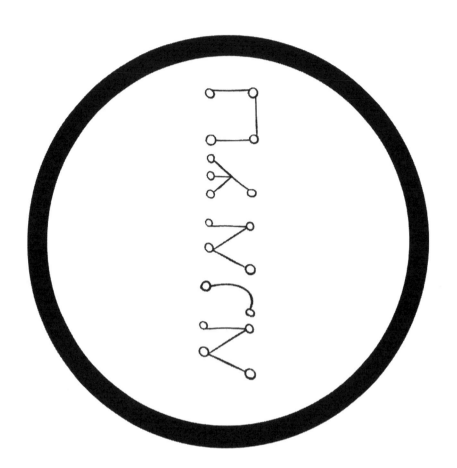

56. Poiel: Increase Success

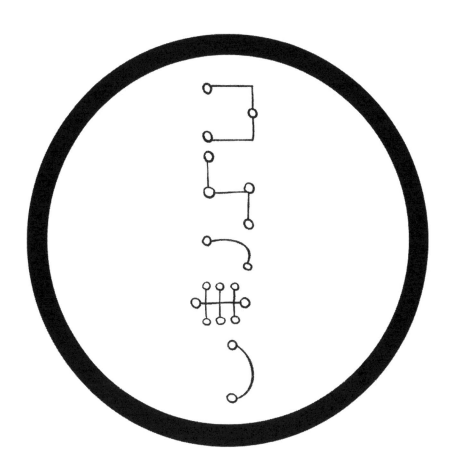

57. Nememiah: Reward for Effort

58. Yeyilel: Ease Grief

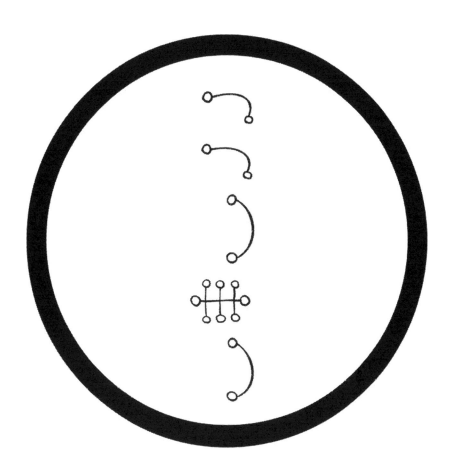

59. Harachel: Invest Wisely

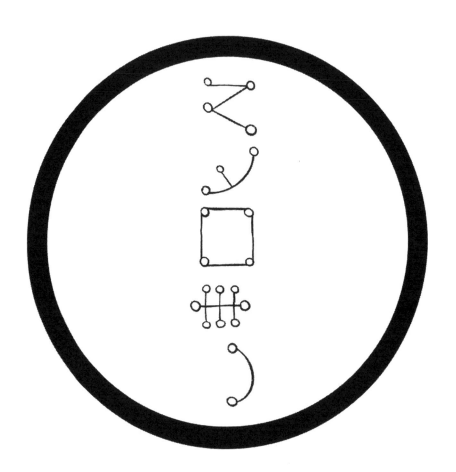

60. Metzerel: Ease Suffering

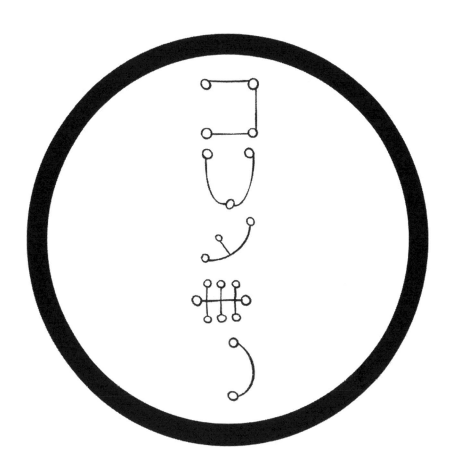

61. Umabel: Improve Friendship

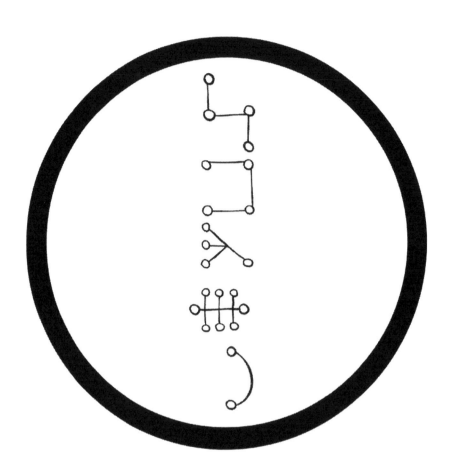

62. Yahahel: Keep Secrets

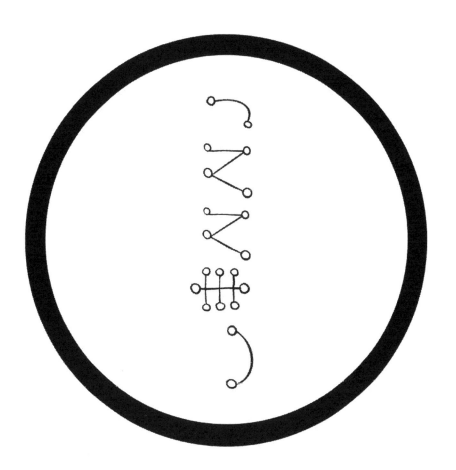

63. Anuel: Protect Your Business or Job

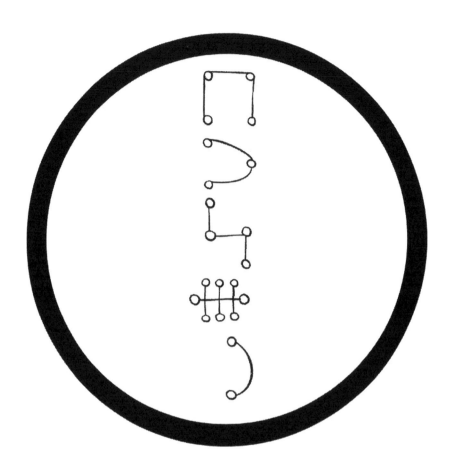

64. Machiel: Popularity

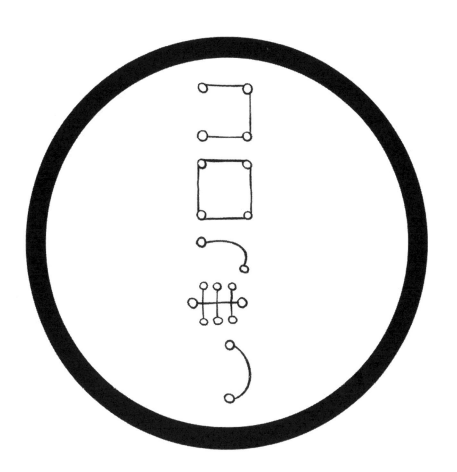

65. Damebiah: Protect Against Curses

66. Menakel: Sleep Well

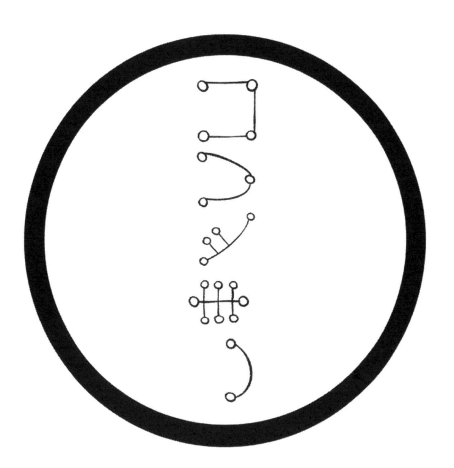

67. Iyahel: Make a Breakthrough

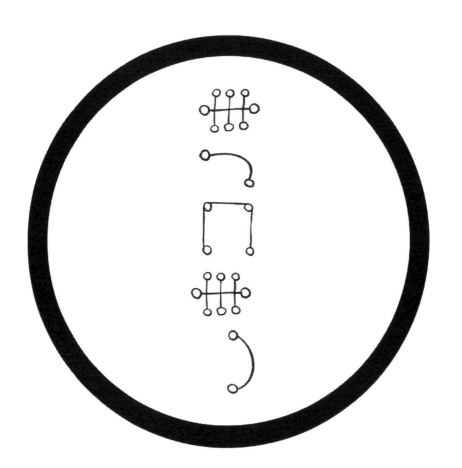

68. Chavuiah: Inspired Solutions

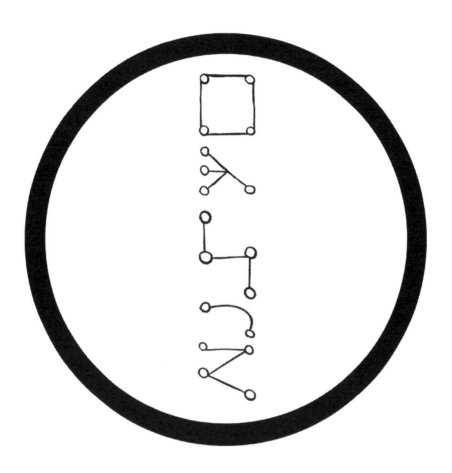

69. Rahahel: Find Lost Objects

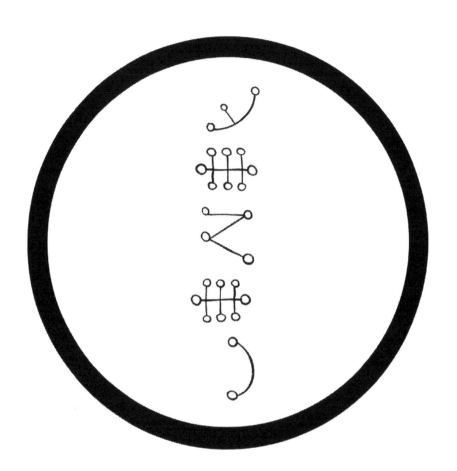

70. Yabamiah: Obtain Perspective

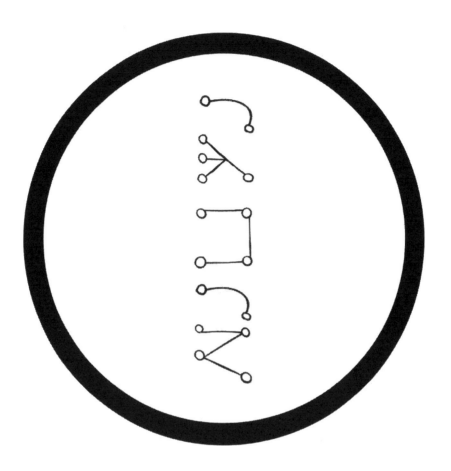

71. Hayiel: Recover from Exhaustion

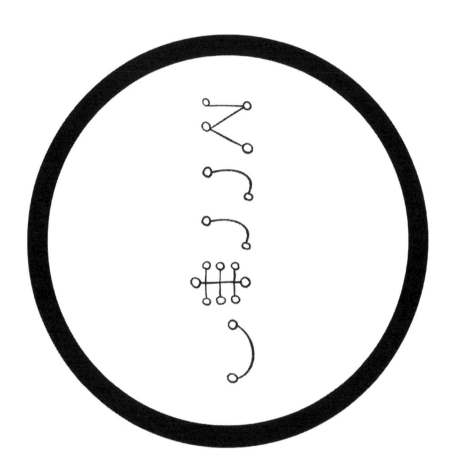

72. Mumiah: Complete a Project

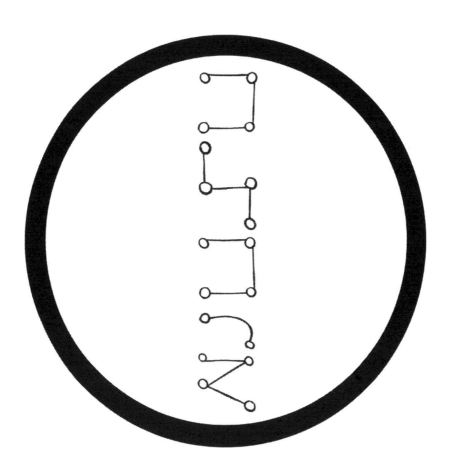

How Magick is Shared

by Chris Wood

Thank you for buying this book. I am proud to release another book by Ben Woodcroft. He is undoubtedly one of the finest occult writers of modern times.

If you are looking for more background information, please see Ben's book, *The Angel Overlords*, which contains one of the best summaries of modern occult developments, some fascinating and amusing history, as well as lots of practical magick.

At *The Power of Magick Publishing*, we believe we have now published a few modern classics. I hope to keep publishing occult books in the coming years. I appreciate your support, as do the authors.

As a reader, I hope you get good value from our books. If you enjoyed *Angelic Trance Magick*, please write a review on Amazon or Goodreads so that people know we are doing something worthwhile. In the modern era of publishing, it is the only way we are able to continue. Thank you.

Chris Wood

The Power of Magick Publishing

www.thepowerofmagick.com

Other books from The Power of Magick

7 Occult Money Rituals by *Henry Archer*
This book contains simple rituals that bring the money you desire. No demons, no darkness. You get powerful, light magick, using angelic names and sigils. Your wants and needs are converted into reality through the power of magick.

Angelic Sigils, Seals and Calls by *Ben Woodcroft*
Discover 142 Angels and Archangels, and the secret sigils, keys, and calls that let you make instant contact with them.

The Angel Overlords by *Ben Woodcroft*
These angels can generate an energy state within you that attracts what you want and repels what you don't want. It is a pure form of magick that works quickly and safely.

Angelic Protection Magick by *Ben Woodcroft*
Angelic protection is gentle, calm, and kind, yet powerful, subtle, and cunning. This bright, white magick can make your enemies tremble with awe while keeping you safe with the power of light.

The Magick of Angels and Demons by *Henry Archer*
Combine the magick of angels and demons, and you get an unheard-of way to control your life. The Union of Power is a priceless method for tasking the angels and demons without any sacrifice or lengthy rituals.

Lucifer and The Hidden Demons by *Theodore Rose*
There are more than 100 demons in this book, and most are unknown outside of the secret orders. You will have the ability to work with hundreds of unique powers.